ABBACADABRA!

The magic of Abba has swept the world: they have had No. 1 hits in every European country, in Australia and in America; in Britain they were once presented with 32 gold, platinum and silver discs in one ceremony; their world record sales topped 40 million in 1976 – more than anyone since The Beatles; and their charm and Swedish good looks have captured hearts wherever they have appeared.

At the centre of this whirlwind of success are four young people with doubts and fears, loves and hates, problems and passions. Anni-Frid was the despised daughter of a Norwegian girl and a German soldier; Benny's past is clouded by a secret girlfriend who cares for his two children; Bjorn is a frustrated intellectual, a dropped-out undergraduate who has to remember to smile on stage, involved in a running battle with critics who say his music is plastic; Agnetha is a country girl who hid her shyness beneath a mask of arrogance.

And there is a fifth member of Abba: the shadowy Stikkan Andersson, an ex-schoolteacher who turned Swedish show-business upside-down with his controversial methods and his relentless hunger for success.

Their problems, their secrets, their love for each other: here for the first time is the whole story behind the new Beatles – the truth about Abba.

THE AUTHORS

Harry Edgington, 35, is a former *Daily Sketch* reporter who has served as Hollywood correspondent for the *Daily Mail,* the *Daily Mirror*, and *The Sun*. Now a freelance journalist and author, he has co-authored *Shake A Pagoda Tree* – the autobiography of Mike and Bernie Winters – *How To Survive in the Nick, The Story of the Goons* and *Bomb Squad*. He splits his working life between London, Los Angeles, and various parts of Europe.

Peter Himmelstrand, 40, spans triple careers as a journalist, lyric writer, composer, and record producer. He was music columnist of *Expressen*, Sweden's leading evening newspaper, for fifteen years. Among the artistes he has penned hit records for are three members of Abba, Bjorn Ulvaeus, Benny Andersson, and Agnetha Faltskog. He has been a close confidant of the Abba team and of their 'fifth member', Stikkan Andersson, since their earliest days in showbusiness. Peter lives in Huddinge, Sweden, with his girlfriend, Annika, and two children from a previous marriage.

ABBA

Harry Edgington
and
Peter Himmelstrand

Everest Books Ltd

4 Valentine Place, London SE1

Published in Great Britain by Everest Books Ltd, 1977

A paperback original

ISBN 0905018 745

Printed in Great Britain by
The Anchor Press Ltd, Tiptree, Essex

CONTENTS

CHAPTER ONE

ANNI-FRID

The more polite friends of the young Norwegian girl ignored her when they passed in the street. The others either swore at her or spat on the pavement. Her crime? She had fallen in love with a German officer, one of the army which had kept Norway under its heel during the wartime years, and was expecting his child.

It was 1945, just after the end of the war, and this was Narvik, a town in the far north of Norway which had seen the ignominious flight of the British and French soldiers in 1940 and since then gone through all the pain of being a defensive outpost of the Third Reich. The German occupiers – and their brutal methods – were hated and feared by the local population. For four years, they had no choice but to bend the knee to the invaders. But when Synni Lyngstad, an innocent nineteen-year-old, came face to face with that officer, Alfred Haase, he seemed somehow different to the others. To her, he was a young man forced to leave his loved ones to take up a duty he abhorred. She listened to him talking about the home and parents he missed, his friends. He was different to the other jackbooted officers strutting around town. They started meeting in what they thought were clandestine encounters. In fact, everybody in town knew about them and talked about Synni and her German lover. Her relatives tried to warn her. 'You must keep away from him,' they said. 'He may be kind and gentle, but he is a German. The war will be over soon, but no-one here will forget this business.' Sadly, they were right. At the end of the war, the young Alfred was shipped back to Germany. Before he left, he promised to return to marry his Synni. But he never came back.

Their child, a daughter, was born on 15 November 1945, and named Anni-Frid after Synni's grandmother. That winter was the coldest Europe had known for years, but the ice was warmer than the feelings the people of Narvik had for Synni – and her daughter. They still hated in Norway, and the locals spat out the name given by Norwegians to all the babies born to Norwegian girls from the German soldier fathers – 'tysk-barn', which means 'German child'.

For nearly two years, Synni Lyngstad waited in Narvik for her wartime lover to return. Her mother watched her slowly pining away amidst her unhappiness and loneliness and the hate heaped on her. Synni died when she was just twenty-one. The grandmother realised that little Anni-Frid, with the tag 'German child', would have a miserable time if she stayed to grow up in Narvik. So she gathered a few possessions and took the girl to Sweden, where no-one would know of her beginnings and where she could live a normal life. They moved from one small country town to another, the grandmother earning enough to keep them by working as a seamstress. For years they were on the move, until finally they settled in the village of Torshälla. This is where Anni-Frid grew up.

When Anni-Frid talks about these days, a misty look comes over her face and you can see her feeling the suffering her mother went through. 'I feel so sad for her,' she says. 'To think of a young girl having all that unhappiness. But I do not blame my father. I don't think it was his fault. I think he was as much a victim of the war as she was. I would like to have met him. I am sure he wanted to come back to Norway to marry her but that something happened to prevent him doing it. I have tried to find him but that is obviously very difficult. I don't think he ever got back to Germany. From what I have been able to find out, I believe his troopship was sunk off Denmark in one of the last actions of the war. So while my mother was waiting for him to return, his body was probably at the bottom of the sea.

'I have been back to Narvik since, to visit my relatives. People don't hate there any more and it is hard to imagine how they looked to my mother. But to them, for her to love a German was absolutely inexcusable. After all these years, we perhaps find it difficult to believe that essentially kind people could carry so much resentment, but then we do not know what it is like to be occupied by a foreign army.'

The young Anni-Frid was brought up as a Swedish citizen, and she now considers herself very much Swedish, rather than Norwegian. Because she could never remember her real mother, she has always called her grandmother 'Mama', and still does.

Anni-Frid has fond memories of those childhood days with her grandmother. 'She was always so kind to me, and encouraged me in anything I did,' she recalls. 'I particularly remember the long, dark, and cold winter evenings when we would sit together round the fire and she would teach me to sing old Swedish and Norwegian folk songs. It was Mama who encouraged me to sing, and it was she who helped me to discover that I could sing, and enjoyed singing.'

At the age of ten, Anni-Frid sang her first engagement. On stage at the local village hall, entertaining the other children – and a few of the adults, too. She did not have a trace of stage nerves. However, later she was to find that her nervousness was to grow in proportion to the engagement and its importance.

She moved fluently on to her debut as a dance band singer in a restaurant club at Eskilstuna, a town near Stockholm that she and her grandmother moved to. Anni-Frid was just thirteen years old, officially too young to appear in such an establishment. She overcame this small problem by lying about her age, adding three years on. She got away with it because she looked mature enough and, perhaps more important, her singing matched this impression. It was the true beginning of her apprenticeship.

Within a couple of years, she had her own dance band – The Anni-Frid Four – which backed her singing in the local nightspots around Eskilstuna, three or four nights a week.

'They were really fun days,' she remembers. 'We were getting paid, but I was singing for fun, because I really enjoyed it. And the band were always so relaxed and happy. They had that carefree air of bands, which you only find in small supper clubs. There was no great pressure on them, and their playing – and their smiling faces – betrayed the contentment they felt.'

The bass player and leader of the band was a furniture salesman, Ragnar Fredriksson. Anni-Frid liked the way he handled the musicians. She also liked him. They started to date, and fell in love. They got engaged and, in the Swedish fashion, started living together. At the age of sixteen, she had a son, Hans. The year after they married and later had another child, a daughter, Lise-Lotte. She also kept up her musical partnership with Ragnar, and they toured together, leaving the children in the care of her grandmother.

When she was eighteen she entered an amateur singing contest in the nearby town of Vasteras. The tall, beautiful girl with a red dress matching her reddish-brown hair, knocked the judges out with her powerful rendering of the Spanish song 'Besame Mucho'. Called up to collect her prize, she shyly told how she had learned the melody on her honeymoon in the Canary Islands. The lyrics she learned from a record, and a Spanish-speaking friend translated the words for her. Leading the applause in the audience was Ragnar, who was so happy for her. He had no way of knowing that this victory was the first of a chain of events which were inevitably to take Anni-Frid away from him. For Anni-Frid was, and still is, a girl with big ambitions. The band, she knew, was adequate for her appearances in the restaurants, but she also knew that if she was to make her way in showbusiness – as she was sure she could – she would have to work with better musicians. The better musicians were in Stockholm, and it was to Stockholm she went in 1967 to take part in an all-Sweden 'New Faces' talent contest organised by the childrens' charity, Barnens Dag. She won, singing a ballad called 'A Day Off'.

Afterwards the compere asked her: 'What are you going to do now?'

A very happy Anni-Frid answered: 'I'm going home to sleep.'

'Oh, no, you are not,' said the compere. 'Outside this door is a car which is going to take you to appear on a television show.'

The astonished and bewildered Anni-Frid was whisked into a television chat show, where she was asked what job she did. Her answer was: 'I am married and have two children. That is my profession.' That was not to be true for very much longer.

She got on to a television show and suddenly everybody wanted the honey-voiced Anni-Frid to sing for them. She went on tours round the *folkparks*, the summer entertainment centres which were set up at the turn of the century when the Swedish government decided that every town and village should have its own outdoor amusements. This time Anni-Frid recalls as 'a long-term exercise in keeping on the move and keeping fit – but it was also a lot of fun'. She said: 'Despite the rigours of the hectic travelling – because the *folkparks* are spread far and wide all over the country – and the poor facilities the artistes had to put up with at some of the smaller centres, I always enjoyed those tours. I suppose you can compare the *folkparks* circuit to the old music halls in England and vaudeville in the United States, where performers learned their business. It's a hard school, but a good one. And, of course, Sweden is a lovely country to travel in, especially in the summer. So my memory tells me those were some of the best days of my life. But I do wonder if it is a case of my memory being kind to history. What they certainly were, were very relaxed days, with none of the pressures of business that I have to face now.'

The hardest part of working, for Anni-Frid, was being away from her children for long stretches. She said later: 'I miss them very much and it hurts me to be forced to leave them for so long, but I see them as much as I can, and we really get on well together. Fortunately, they have a good father in Ragnar, and they are very happy.'

Ragnar, for his part, was very understanding. He said: 'I am not afraid of playing second fiddle to Anni-Frid's career. If she has the chance to be successful, she must take it. I would never stand in her way.' Leaving the children behind was an awfully big wrench for her. Everybody could see the sadness in her eyes when she spoke about being away from them.

Despite her unhappiness about leaving the children, Anni-Frid felt she must go and live in Stockholm to spend her time at the hub of the music business if she was to further her career. So she said goodbye to her husband and two children, leaving them in the old wooden villa they had shared, and took the train the seventy miles to Stockholm. There, she found a small flat and settled into a life which, outside working hours, meant a lot of loneliness. She said later: 'Nobody knows the strain I was under at this time. I'd present a public image of a smiling, happy singer. But underneath, I felt a lot of sadness. I'm sorry to say that many people who should have known better were very nasty about what I had done. They said I didn't care about my children, and abandoned them to come to Stockholm to work with the big boys. They could not have been more wrong. I had not abandoned them. In fact, I thought of bringing them to Stockholm with me. Then I looked round my tiny flat and realised that that was a silly thought. There was no room, and I would not have been able to look after them properly. I did the right thing. Ragnar looked after them well and they were better off with him than stuck in a poky little place in the big city with me. I tried not to think about missing them, but it was very hard. I tell you, I shed quite a few tears over them in those days.'

Although Anni-Frid thought the world of her children, her marriage to Ragnar was not a very good one. She really thought she was doing the best thing for the children. So it was really the combination of a marriage going off the boil and a career hotting up which made her leave them. She was so upset that people said such unpleasant things about her going away. The authors believed her when she said: 'It is very hard for me to do it, but I can leave the children because I know they will have a better time with their father than with me.' Her decision did mean that she got into the mainstream of Swedish showbusiness and she completed a very full apprenticeship.

This took Anni-Frid through the full course of appearances in restaurants, melody festivals, and reviews. Her records sold well and she became a regular visitor to the Swedish best-selling charts, though the knockers claimed that her singing appealed to only a narrow audience. She got the opportunity to work with many of the most popular artistes and actors in Scandinavia, and she took part in international song contests around the world, including two in Japan and Venezuela. Appearances on the popular Swedish Television programme 'Hyland's Corner' ensured her nationwide recognition and set her firmly on the road to becoming, in her own right, one of Sweden's premier singers.

CHAPTER TWO

BENNY

If anybody asks the jovial, bearded, and ever-so-slightly rotund Benny Andersson about his education, he has a smiling and ready reply for them. 'I have a driver's licence,' he says. It is his benign cover for a schooling that never got on the move, let alone reached the dizzy heights. The only subject he could handle with any ability was English, which, in stark contrast to the other subjects, he absorbed like a sponge. But his consuming interest in life was, and still is, music. Not that he can read music. Like other academic subjects, that is too much like hard work, and the written theory is a continuing mystery to him. Music to him meant playing: playing anything he could lay his hands on – an accordion, harmonica, whatever came his way. He was fortunate in having a father and grandfather who both had a musical bent and were determined to cultivate the budding talent in young Benny. They did so by giving him a piano-accordion.

Born in the suburbs of Stockholm, on 16 December, 1946, Benny drifted through his school life with the air of sleepy detachment which has so often characterized him when he comes up against something he is not really interested in. He left school at fifteen without taking any of the leaving examinations and settled down to concentrate full time on music. The mysteries of the accordion were soon overcome by his inquisitive musical fingers, and he progressed to a piano which was brought into the house as a further encouragement to him.

Benny recalls: 'I think coming from a musical family gives you something in life that everybody else should feel envious of. My grandfather and father were just like me. They would try any, but *any*, musical instrument that they could find, whether it was the piano-accordion they gave me, or a flute, or a fiddle. I guess I just inherited whatever they had. They loved folk music, the older and cornier the better. I learned a lot of the old tunes from them and my early playing had a definite folk flavour about it. I'm glad to say that is all in the past now.'

He was two years out of school and still trying to decide which part of the business world would benefit from his presence before any outsider recognised the talent which his family had known was there from the very beginning. The meantime had been filled in with musing about the future and playing piano with a group whose name has long since drifted into the annals of anonymity. But it was his membership of this group which was to lift him from the doldrums and plant him where his ability could be used. The group had to travel to an engagement, and as this was unusual – no-one normally *asked* them along – they had to look around for someone with the transport to get them to their rare playdate. Their thoughts lit upon Svenne Hedlund, a singer with a group called Hep Stars, who was the proud possessor of a sizeable van. Svenne was free that night and agreed to drive them in his van, which was old but vast, and perfect for the task of carrying a group and their mountain of equipment. Svenne stayed to watch the show, and saw immediately that Benny was head and shoulders above his partners. Shortly after, Hep Stars lost their organ player and Svenne's thoughts returned to Benny. He asked Benny, who accepted with alacrity, realising that his first group was on that short slide into oblivion.

Svenne peers back into the past to recount: 'Benny was a good musician, but he wasn't like the rest of us in Hep Stars at all. He had neat crewcut hair and wore a tie. He was so clean and nice. We all had long hair, and looked a pretty wild lot. And we thought ties were for wearing at funerals. But I'll give it to Benny. He made the transformation in a few months. He grew his hair long and looked as wild as the rest of us.'

With the twin sex-appeal power of Svenne and Benny in the van, Hep Stars became the biggest rock group in Sweden, in fact the biggest pop music happening in that country till Abba came along. Benny remembers: 'When I look back at Hep Stars, I realise we used to play a sort of country and western with a German beat, if you can imagine that. At the time, though, we thought we were an up-to-the-minute rock group; and luckily that's what everybody else seemed to think we were.'

Benny was looked upon as the newcomer to the group for a long time by the other four members, who had all been in on the founding of Hep Stars. It didn't worry him, as long as he could play. As always, Benny just seemed to be floating through life. He was always laughing and joking and always, but always, seemed so content. Nothing worried him and he didn't seem to have it in him to be able to get angry. When everybody else in Hep Stars was getting uptight and gritting their teeth, he would be sitting there, calm as an old man on a park bench. All the problems of the group just passed straight over his head and it was as if he didn't even notice they were there. And the group had plenty of problems. They drove the recording technicians mad because they were pathologically incapable of getting to a recording studio together and on time. Often, they were hours late because some of them had overslept. Then they would argue backwards and forwards, and shout and scream about whether a number should be done this way or that. And in the middle of it all, the unruffled Benny would be playing a gentle tune on his harmonica. He just had to be seen to be believed.

Hep Stars moved from playing youth clubs around Stockholm to jet into a bigger orbit. Their following built up quickly, they started getting bookings up and down the country and, suddenly, they were stars, looked upon as Sweden's answer to The Beatles. Which they weren't. But it was a comforting title to carry, even if the bank manager was totally unimpressed. Their tours started taking in the open-air theatres of the *folkparks* during the short but sweet Swedish summer. Their crossover into more adventurous pop music coincided with a rise in their earnings. But Benny never seemed interested in money. All he wanted out of life was to play music, and he was now getting plenty of opportunity to do that, so he was delighted. The earnings from his work have always seemed secondary to Benny. Benny would play for the rest of his life for no money. He's the sort of person who is addicted to instruments. If there is one around, he'll be there, playing it. He turned up at hotels on working tours and went straight to the piano to knock out a tune. It wouldn't matter to him that he was going to spend the rest of the night working on a piano. And if Benny is missing suddenly from a party or company, you know where he has gone. Find the musical instrument in the house, and you'll find him.

Not long after Benny teamed up with Hep Stars, they were putting a bunch of tunes together to make a long playing record, but found that they were one short. None of them could think of a suitable tune to fit in the last slot. Benny saved the day after he came up to Svenne to quietly whisper, in a most unselfconfident manner: 'I've written a song, and I think we can use.'

'I hope we can,' said Svenne. 'It could be just what we need.' It was. The song was 'No Response', which was truly a misnomer, because it was a very big 1965 hit for Hep Stars.

However, this success did not transform Benny into a bundle of energy. 'In fact, when it came to knuckling down to work, he was bordering on the lazy,' said Svenne. 'We had to wait a long time before he came up with another song for us. Strange that he seemed to be playing music all the time, which was such a joy to him that it wasn't like work. But when it needed some concentration and some effort to put a song together, it was always something he was going to get round to later.'

Benny did eventually write more for Hep Stars, and turned out many of their hits of the 1960s. In fact, two of his songs, 'Wedding', which he wrote with Svenne Hedlund, and 'Sunny Girl' were instrumental in enhancing the reputation of the group. By the time he was nineteen he had written just three tunes in his life, but they had all got into the song charts, and two of them were in the top ten at the same time. 'Wedding' went to number one.

His method of songwriting has not changed over the years. First he would tinkle about on the piano until he found some chords that pleased him. Then he'd string them together to complete the melody. When that was done, his imagination would go walkabout to search for lyrics which matched the mood of the music. 'Wedding' got its title because Benny thought the opening bars were like the church music he had heard at weddings. 'That's because it starts out like a church organ,' he said. 'I played it to a church organist who thought it sounded like a wedding march. So I wrote the lyric about a wedding. And, although English isn't my native language, I find writing in it easy enough if I have something to write about.' His next step was to get someone to write the notes down for him; this is something he still has to do for, even now, he has not learned to write music.

Benny quickly established himself as the most talented musician in the group. He also rapidly challenged Svenne Hedlund as the sex symbol of the group, the one their growing band of screaming teenagers shoutest loudest for. This was because Benny looked shy and nice and had that generous smile.

Benny was, and is, modest and gentle and loveable, a big, warm, cuddly guy. But he did like being an idol for the teenagers and all the adulation that went with it. What he didn't like about it was that it restricted his second favourite hobby – going to restaurants. They couldn't go openly to a restaurant, because they would be mobbed. So he and Svenne indulged themselves with big American cars, and it became a familiar sight to see them turn up separately and make a dash into the concert hall, avoiding the flesh-tearing clutches of the fans.

When he wasn't doing one of those lightning dashes, Benny was his usual lethargic self. A friend recalls: 'Whenever I called him when he was on tour, he was in bed. He always seemed to be tired.' He teamed up with a songwriter called Lars Berhagen to write more hit songs for Hep Stars, who by now were winning one gold record after another and chalking up 100,000 sales of individual records – very high totals for Sweden in those days. Said Benny: 'It's easier for two to write a song, especially if you are a bit lazy. You can push each other along.' Lars Berhagen, playing the guitar to Benny's piano, certainly had a remarkable method of keeping Benny on the right track. If Lars didn't like what he was playing, he would go up and bang the piano lid down on his fingers. Amazingly, Benny remembers: 'We met each other every day for a year without getting angry at each other.' The melodies were still coming easily to Benny, but he was having the usual struggle to find the lyrics. Once, he and Lars wrote what they thought would be a big smash hit for Cilla Black. Unfortunately, she never got round to hearing it.

The Hep Stars began their own publishing and business company to exploit and market the songs they were writing. They also had grandiose plans to publish other people's music and make their records. The company was called Hep House, and it was the biggest flop Benny has ever been associated with.

When Benny had just started in pop music, it was for fun. Only when the tunes he wrote in his happy-go-lucky way became successful did he take the business more seriously. Up until then he had just been fooling around. Looking at the track record of Hep House, it is clear that Benny would have been better off tackling pop in his old, nonchalant way. Hep House showed the pop stars that they were amateurs in business. They lost their money faster than they made it. They invested in the production of a film which was to be made in Africa, but not an inch of film was shot. They paid for a trip to America, for reasons which no-one now can quite remember. They also were induced to hire a private plane to take them to London, on the promise that a recording there would inject the 'British sound' and new life into their music. But there was no mystical secret to be found in that basement Soho studio. The record was never released.

At the end of this foray into big business, Benny was much

wiser, but also much poorer. The company went bankrupt, leaving Benny with a monumental tax bill to meet on his earlier earnings. He was to earn virtually nothing from the next few songs he wrote because the taxman's demands were always on the doormat.

A problem of a different nature was waiting for Benny. In the summer of 1966 he had broken off a four year engagement to Christina Grönvall, a pretty red-haired girl he had met at school. They had lived together most of that time and Christina bore him two children, a boy called Peter, and a girl, Helena. The romance had been a closely guarded secret because these were the days when it was considered anathema for news of a pop star's girlfriend to get out. A few months after the break-up, Christina challenged him in a Swedish magazine article: 'Tell them about me and the kids, the family you don't have room for in the glittery world of a pop idol.' She said Benny had left their flat at Valingby, near Stockholm, and the only contact the children had had with their father since then was through the Hep Stars records. Christina said: 'He ended our engagement very quickly. Just one phone call. No explanations.' Benny kept quiet about her and the children, she said, because he did not want his fans to find out. 'His fans would be jealous and Benny thought this would damage his career,' said Christina. 'To go around with a baby carriage in his company was unthinkable. Once I followed the Hep Stars on tour, but I had to travel behind in the orchestra bus and hide during the show.' But some fans knew about the relationship. The telephone rang one night just after Christina had put the children to bed. A girl's voice asked for Benny, but Christina said he was away on tour. The girl asked who she was talking to and Christina told the girl her name. A minute later the girl telephoned again. This time she was hysterical. When Christina answered, she screamed: 'Keep away from Benny.' Benny would not discuss the relationship at the time, but he has talked about it to friends, and made it clear he was shocked that people should take such an avid interest in his personal affairs. This sort of thing is common in Sweden, where couples live together often for many years before they marry. Sometimes they break up, and the girl is left to look after one or two children on her own. Benny told friends he was surprised so much fuss was made about it. He was also disappointed that people wanted to pry into a part of his life which he considered private and entirely his own business. He still feels that way.

CHAPTER THREE

BJORN

Bjorn Ulvaeus started a folk singing quartet with a bunch of school friends to while away the time until he went to college. It was just an exercise in fun for him, but his proud mother thought she was witnessing the birth of a musical miracle. She dreamed up a name for the group and, without telling them, entered the boys for a radio talent contest. They didn't win, but listening to the show was a man whose instant belief in the four youngsters would project them, within the space of a few weeks, into the mainstream of Swedish showbusiness.

During the dying days of the Second World War, Bjorn was born on 25 April, 1945, in the west coast city of Gothenberg. When he was eleven years old, his family moved to the tiny and beautiful east coast town of Vastervik – a name meaning 'West Bay' in English. He learned to play the guitar fooling around with a group playing skiffle, the raw folk music which was sweeping the world at that time. At seventeen, Bjorn called three of his musical pals together and told them he wanted to form a Dixieland jazz band. The idea was to play dates to raise money for the school. Now he admits: 'It wasn't really a very serious undertaking, though I think I managed to give some people the impression that it was. For my part, I wanted something to get involved in while I was waiting to go to college. My talk to the guys about jazz and all that stuff was a bit ostentatious. I didn't know much about it, and our music came out more like American folk music, in the style of the Kingston Trio, who were a very big group then. I'm not sure if we realised it at the time, but we were probably copying them.' Whatever the source of their style, the people of Vastervik liked them, and the boys stayed together. Then, one day their practice sessions at Bjorn's home stirred his mother to fill in a form, entering them for an 'Opportunity Knocks' style programme on Swedish Radio, the government-run equivalent of the BBC. The form requested the name of the performers, but the group at that time had no name. So the inventive Mrs Ulvaeus borrowed the English versions of their town name to write in 'The West Bay Singers'.

'I was astonished when I heard she had entered us,' says Bjorn. 'At first I wanted to withdraw us from the contest, because I was in no way sure that we were ready for that sort of thing. Then I reconsidered. I thought: "Why shouldn't we be in it? We're not that bad. We might have a chance. Who knows?" And the name had a pleasant folksy ring about it, which matched the style of our performance, where we sang most of our songs in unison. I told the others about the entry, and they showed none of my reserve. They thought it was a great idea to compete.'

A review of the programme, mentioning that The West Bay Singers were entered, and that they would be singing in both Swedish and English, appeared in a newspaper read by Bengt Bernhag, a prolific discoverer of Swedish talent. He was a wise old cat who had that uncanny knack of spotting the potential of performers which more suave, but less intuitive, competitors lacked. He produced a couple of girl singers who no-one else had been prepared to do anything for. They became chart-toppers. He launched an old trumpet player who specialised in folk music. Everybody in the business laughed – especially Bengt when the trumpeter's records were big hits. He always managed to have the last laugh, but he never rubbed his successes in. He was ever the self-effacing, modest, and polite, and carefully disguised dynamo. Bengt liked the name 'The West Bay Singers', and resolved to listen to the radio show. He found he also liked the simple, honest and straightforward presentation of the group. He mentioned the group to the boss of his organisation, an irreverent, establishment-rocking, and energetic music publisher and producer, Stikkan Andersson. They contacted Bjorn to ask for a demonstration tape. This came up to expectations, so Bengt and Stikkan asked the group to come up to their Stockholm studios for a more precise and exacting test. They sailed through this, with Bengt's and Stikkan's approval registering in their beaming faces.

Bjorn recalls: 'That was a very nervous day for all of us, believe me. From a nowhere, nothing, group doing schoolboy gigs we were suddenly under the searching gaze of two of the best pros in the music business. But their calm manner in dealing with us – they must have realised we would be very much on edge – helped to cool us down and we played and sang well that day.'

The first thing Stikkan Andersson did for the group was to change their name. The American Hootenanny music was starting to emerge and looked like being the new worldwide rage. For a while he'd carried the name for a group, which he was about to present to Bjorn and his friends. It was 'The Hootenanny Singers'. Not that their music was even remotely Hootenanny. It was just a commercial, infectious, and memorable name which Stikkan was convinced would help them. Stikkan said recently: 'The West Bay name was nice, but very parochial and olde worlde. Not the sort of title for a group of young guys who, I felt sure, were going to hammer their way into the charts.'

So 'The Hootenanny Singers' they became, and Bjorn recalls the irony of that decision. 'A few weeks before we didn't even have a name,' he said. 'Then my Mum – good old Mum, it all happened because of her and I often find myself saying a few silent words of thanks to her – picked our first name. It was that name which drew the attention of Bengt and got us into the studios. And the next thing is we were given a new name for our first recording. Strange, but that's just the way it was.'

First record for The Hootenanny Singers was a perfect foil for their melancholy unison singing. It carried the wordy and strange title of 'I'm Waiting at the Charcoal Kiln' and was a sad old Swedish song about people who worked in the forest.

Immediately it was a success. Exhilarating for the boys and a memorable moment for Stikkan Andersson; he had just launched his own label, Polar Records, and Hootenanny were the first artistes to go out on that label. Said Stikkan: 'I felt the group had good potential, if they got the right guidance. They blended so well and the blond, good-looking Bjorn was a natural, and a great lead for them. But an immediate smash success was more than any of us had dared hope for.'

In 1964, with his college aspirations temporarily shelved, Bjorn and The Hootenanny Singers went on tour around Sweden, including the inevitable *folkparks*. 'At the time those *folkparks* tours seemed the hardest of all,' says Bjorn. 'The conditions for the artistes were appalling, and we were on the move all the time. But, in retrospect, I think we learned a lot and the tours did afford us the pleasure of seeing all of the country.' The Hootenanny Singers quickly built up a solid following amongst both teenagers and older people. 'We didn't get mobbed or anything like that, but that sort of idolisation I can do without,' says Bjorn.

After a year on tour, Bjorn got the feeling that perhaps the other members of the group were not as dedicated to making a musical career as he was. They started doing odd jobs, working in their father's firms, doing book-keeping, or selling cars. The truth was that the other members of the group were essentially small-town boys who were a little frightened by the sudden success. Bjorn, on the other hand, quickly outgrew the small-town mentality. If he goes back to Vastervik now, he feels a stranger. So Bjorn started to have his doubts about his own showbusiness career and took up his place at the University of Stockholm to read Economics and Law. This phase was not to last long. He did not seem to take university life so seriously. He was always hopping from one course to another, as if he could not make up his mind where to settle. His heart was really in the music business and he used to say he thought he could make it as an international artiste. But he felt he should hedge his bets by studying at the University in case the group fell apart. The courses were easy for him. He was always a bit of an intellectual, and had excelled in most subjects at school.

The stirring confidence of Stikkan Andersson and the fatherly advice of Bengt Bernhag persuaded Bjorn where his future lay. Stikkan told him that since starting his music business, he had determined that one day he would break out of the straitjacket of limitations which faced most people in the business in Sweden. He was going to launch an international star, he confided. And that star he felt sure was Bjorn.

Bjorn could not have fallen into a better set-up to assure his future. Bengt was a great music technician, and taught him all he knew. In fact, he always looked on Bjorn as his son. Which, in a way, he was. For without Bengt, Bjorn superstar might never have been created. And Stikkan showed him the business end of things, something Bjorn took to like a duck to water. A friend says: 'Stikkan has always been a businessman *par excellence*, and the only mind I have met that I think could ever make a match for him is Bjorn's. He is a cold and analysing type of person. If you watch him when he is working on business or the production of a record, you can almost hear his mind ticking over, just like a precision machine. Why, he is so mechanical, he even has to remind himself to smile on-stage.'

The Hootenanny Singers went back on tour, and they were to stay together as a group for years, turning out a considerable number of hits on the way. However, they were not wealthy enough to travel in style yet. An old Volvo with their double bass strapped on top was the sign that they had arrived in town. Even the car didn't belong to the group. They had to borrow that from one of their fathers.

Bjorn always stood out in the group; he was always the anchor man. Bengt Bernhag picked out songs which he could make as a solo artiste, a career which he nurtured while Bjorn was still with The Hootenanny Singers. He gave up the University, and dedicated himself to his music career.

He knew The Hootenanny Singers were a limited commodity. Three guys playing guitars and the other a bass while they sing folksy music was not the sort of presentation he could see going onto the world's stage. So he pitched his single-minded and absolute determination into soaking up everything he could about the business and production end, and at the same time made a number of solo records. He used to say that he didn't think The Hootenanny Singers could last, but that he wanted to be sure to be around when they had gone. He was determined to carve himself a long career in the music business. But he did not have just a limited Swedish career in mind. From the very early days he wanted to be a big international name. He really believed that Swedish music and artistes could make it abroad. He would say: 'It hasn't happened before because no-one has really tried. I'm convinced it can be done, and that I can do it.'

That's what Bjorn has – a lot of confidence. Add to that the facts that he is a planner and organiser, with a fantastic capacity for work, and you have a formidable combination. He has his eyes wide open for the faintest glimmer of an opportunity, and when one presents itself, he grabs it with an iron grip.

The Hootenanny Singers continued on the success trail, with their family audiences enjoying their clean-cut college-group air. But, businesslike and cool as he may be offstage, all the sex appeal of the group centred on Bjorn. He was the one the girls went for.

Bjorn was no shrinking violet. When a journalist asked him who was the musical brain behind the group, he immediately replied: 'I am.' Though he did give the other members of the group some credit for consultation. He candidly admitted the problems of four musicians trying to work together, adding: 'We are learning to handle that as we get more experienced. And we are pals, working pals, and because we care about each other, it helps.' Their success, he was also honest enough to admit, did not depend on them being the best musically. 'The most important thing is that we choose the right songs to go with our style,' he said. 'We sing as simply as we can. We have a distinctive combined voice, and it is that which makes us identifiable to people.'

Bowing to public demand, The Hootenanny Singers drifted from folk music to pop. They started singing all their songs in English, which is the international language for pop. 'And, anyway, the kids think songs in Swedish must be old fashioned,' said Bjorn. 'So what can we do? They are the customers, after all. The *folkparks* customers seem to be getting younger and younger all the time, and if it is pop they want, pop it is they'll get. I'm not much on looking into the future, but I do wonder what we'll be doing a few years from now.'

CHAPTER FOUR

AGNETHA

Little Gerhard was a pop singer who retired gracefully into the role of A & R man. Like all of his colleagues around the world, he is regularly plagued by people who would like him to listen to their sister, daughter, or wife's brother. This time it was his cousin. She was singing with a dance band and wanted to make a record. Gerhard asked her to tape one of her shows and send him the tape, which he promised to accord his undiluted attention. The tape duly arrived and Gerhard dutifully sat through all of it. He called up his cousin to say: 'I'm sorry, but I don't think most of that was very good.' However, there was a glimmer of hope. 'I noticed a few snatches of song which were quite good,' he said. 'Why don't you record those songs fully, and I'll listen to them. If you sing like that all the time, I think we can do something.'

There was not a crumb of comfort in this for the cousin. She had to explain: 'But the voice singing those short pieces is not mine. That's a new girl we have singing with the band.' Exit the crestfallen cousin and enter the new girl – the diminutive, blonde, and pretty Agnetha Faltskog.

Agnetha's father, an enthusiastic amateur entrepreneur, used to stage shows in their home town, the lakeside Jonkopping, where she was born on 5 April, 1950. At a tender age, she was introduced to the boards, to sing a song in one of the amateur revues for a gathering of local old folk. 'I shall never forget that start to my career,' she has recounted. 'In the middle of of the song my knickers fell down and the whole of the audience collapsed in hysterical laughter. I was six years old.'

Undaunted by this inauspicious opening, she spent hour after hour with her father and grandfather, playing the family accordion and piano. When she was ten she was given her own piano and very soon she was picking out the notes, concocting her own melodies. She also wrote words to go with the music, beginning with a revue sketch about two trolls – kind Nordic monsters. She returned to the amateur revues to enrapture the audience which had earlier found her so funny. By the time she was fifteen, Agnetha was the regular singer with a dance band orchestra in Jonkopping – looking, despite her age, every inch an accomplished professional. Two years later, she started appearing as the 'guest singer' with other dance bands in the area which is how her voice got on to the tape that ended up in Little Gerhard's office.

Gerhard, an executive with the CBS-Cupol record company, called Agnetha and asked her to send a full tape of one of her songs to him. Her favourite song at that moment was 'I Was So In Love', a heavily sentimental song about a girl who had just lost the big love of her life. That girl was her. She had written the song because she felt so unhappy when her romance with a local boy, Bjorn Lilja, was broken off. She remembers: 'I sat down at the piano and started to play, just to try to forget how unhappy I felt. Half an hour later the melody was finished. I didn't feel any better, but I had what I thought was a lovely and moving song.' Little Gerhard agreed with her opinion. He asked her to come to Stockholm to make a record of her song. So the tiny and nervous Agnetha was put on the train which would take her to the ancient and beautiful capital city of Sweden, which for all Swedes has the simple and reverent title of 'the town'. Her father was there to see her off, with a few final words of advice, and her mother, with a little flutter of concern for her baby daughter. She need not have worried. Agnetha was to prove a formidable match for the big boys of the record world.

She vividly remembers walking into the recording studio for the first time. 'It was the most exciting moment of my life,' she said. 'My heart was in my mouth and I had to consciously make my feet take the steps down to the recording room. Then I heard the string musicians practising my music, the very notes I had picked out on that piano. Suddenly, I was walking on air and floated into the room as if I was on a cloud.'

Little Gerhard was delighted with the two tapes the recording session produced. His boss was somewhat less pleased. He asked him what he thought he was doing wasting the company's time and money on taping a girl from the country who was a complete unknown. When he heard the tapes, he changed his tune. Agnetha was called up to his office, and she immediately sat down to negotiate her own contract. He must have been amazed to find such a tough mind in that tiny, delicate frame. Despite the fact that she was a total newcomer and only seventeen, she was one of the first artistes to have a guaranteed income clause. It gave her a monthly salary for the next three to five years for making records and doing tours.

Within two weeks of release, 'I Was So In Love' was number one on the record charts. Agnetha, who gave up her job as a switchboard operator for a car sales firm and moved to a flat in Stockholm, said: 'I never imagined, that day I sat down to play a few bars of self-condolence, that anybody else would even hear the music. Then a year later it was in the charts. Unbelievable! My boyfriend and I never did patch up our differences, but we are still friends. And I am very grateful to him. If it had not been for him, and if I had not been so unhappy that day, I would never have written that song.' Bjorn Lilja, for his part, was ecstatic about Agnetha's success, and he felt proud that he had inspired the song. He went to see her to offer his congratulations. He wanted to hug her, too, but could not. He had broken both his arms in an accident, and they were in plaster.

Her father, who had already helped her career so much, continued to do so by taking over her business affairs and acting as her manager. She said of him: 'I owe him so much. His patience in spending hours and hours with me at the piano and his continual encouragement have done so much to help me to where I am today. I'll never forget what he did for me.'

From the start, Agnetha developed a reputation as a forceful and highly individual and opinionated girl. The most galling thing about her, to the old established musicians, was that she was usually right. Little Gerhard recalls: 'Right from the start, she was very outspoken about songs, including her own. She said what she thought and she always knew what she wanted. She could recognise a good song if she heard one, and she always knew instinctively if a song would be right for her. Even in those early days, at seventeen years of age, she could listen to a tape once and decide immediately whether she wanted to sing a certain song or not. She had an incredibly wise head on her young shoulders.'

'I Was So In Love' was a gushing, oversentimental song, expressing the high emotional sentiments of a young girl. A strong emotional tension ran through most of her songs, though she once protested: 'Why does everyone think I can only sing about love and that sort of thing? I really can sing other music, too. But songs will always be about love. New and old, it's all alike. It's always like that. I write my love songs under the influence of two flickering candles on my piano. They bring out the romance in me.' Despite her reservations about supercharged emotion in her songs, the Swedish people took her and her music to their hearts. Her two follow-up songs, 'Without You' and 'If Tears Were Gold', were as sentimental as her first – and as successful. She wrote and sang romantic songs because she was a romantically-minded girl, and this just happened to click with the sort of music the public were looking for at that time.

Her forthright manner was to make her social transition from a country town to Stockholm difficult. Despite her apparent bluff self-confidence, she was hiding an inherent shyness. In fact, much of her manner was caused by this. It made her say things she did not mean and she often appeared rude. A friend remembers her early days in Stockholm. 'She had no manners at all, and made all the social *faux pas* you can imagine. She could not even handle a spoon properly. And she was forever saying and doing the wrong things. I remember a time when she was having dinner in a restaurant with some music company people and she embarrassed everybody at the table by shouting at the waiter, complaining about the food, and using coarse language. I'm sure she didn't realise what she was doing, and that the words only tumbled out because she was feeling so shy and insecure. For when she talked to people in private, she was so nice, sweet, and honest. I think that in company she felt so awkward that she over-compensated by being rude and loud. I understand that now she drives interviewers mad. They can't get more than a simple "Yes" or "No" out of her. I think she finally learned that it was better to say nothing than put her foot in it all the time. But she makes up for her public silence in private conversation, when she seems to talk all the time.'

None of this hindered her career, which flowered unchecked. She started appearing on television and set off on the inevitable *folkparks* tours. She included in her growing repertoire 'One Summer With You', which her father had written, and made a special tour to the schools in the Jonkopping area, singing the children a song she had penned about the correct way to brush their teeth. A German record company heard her records, and tried to get her under contract. She turned the offer down, but her popularity in Germany grew, and for a short while she was engaged to a German songwriter, Dietrich Zimmerman. They wrote a number of songs together, but their romance died.

She announced plans to start an acting career, but while she was still making hit records, it was hard for her to take it up. One of her hits, a song called 'Gipsy Friend', which she also wrote herself, was criticised as being racial because it told of the old legends about gipsies. She said: 'I'm sorry if that's what people think. I was only writing a song, that's all.' But she reverted to the sentimental love songs which the public still loved, and which kept her out of the hot water of barbed criticism.

CHAPTER FIVE

A MR BIZ

So the cast was prepared. Four young people, each with their own particular musical ability, were all doing well enough in their own way. But alone they were not going to set the world on fire. Pop experts remember The Beatles in much the same way on the threshold of their career. To light The Beatles' fuel, a torch was needed. He came along, in the form of Brian Epstein, to manage them and ensure their musical immortality. For Anni-Frid, Benny, Bjorn and Agnetha, another such catalyst was waiting in the wings, like a fairy godmother who was going to transform their lives. He was Stikkan Andersson, a former schoolmaster with an impressive zest for business and hard work.

Stikkan Andersson is particularly proud of the fact that he has struggled up to a successful career from a fatherless childhood. His mother was unmarried, a fact that any modern Swede would shrug off as of absolutely no consequence. But in the tiny village of Hova, set in the countryside near Gothenberg, in 1931, long before the sexually enlightened times of post-war Sweden, it was a heavy burden. He felt like an underdog, and claims that this was the prime driving force which made him work hard and determined him to succeed in life. He got an after-school-hours job as a messenger when he was thirteen to save up the money to buy a guitar. Then, as soon as he could play it, he used it to earn more money playing with local dance bands. At fifteen he left school, and immediately started writing songs. His objective? To earn enough money to go to college and train for the career he had set his heart on – as a teacher. He also started writing songs, though, as a self-taught musician, he could not write down the music. When he was eighteen he got his first song published. It went over in a small way, but it was a start and encouraged him to beaver away at more. He wrote a number of comedy songs and included them in a repertoire he built up for tours around the Swedish *folkparks*. Then he teamed up with a friend and for a while they toured as a comedy-singing double act. When Stikkan had saved enough money, he went to college to study and qualify as a teacher, but still managed stage appearances in the evenings. After graduation he got a job teaching chemistry and mathematics in a Stockholm secondary school. Even then, he still spent the evenings writing songs and making occasional appearances.

The end of his teaching career was spelled out by a song he wrote called 'Are You Still In Love With Me, Klas-Goran?' A popular Swedish singer, Lil-Babs, recorded it in 1960 and won a gold record. Stikkan made a lot of money out of it, and realised he could have a big future in showbusiness. He now recalls: 'I enjoyed working at the school, and I had devoted a lot of time and effort to get there. I would rather have done that than stay in small time showbusiness. But if I could get into the really commercial end of the business, who was I to refuse? The music had, anyway, seemed to be getting progressively more important to me, so it was a natural transition. However, it is amusing to look back to see that I concentrated on music to get me through college, and that it was the music which finally took me away from my teaching. That's the way of things, I suppose. What happens in life that you have planned carefully beforehand? Not much.'

All of Stikkan's earlier songs had been published by someone else, and there had been a few minor sellers among them. The 'Klas-Goran' song was something different. It was his first big song, and he used it as the basis of setting himself up as a music publisher. This business he set up in his small house, and he left the school to run it.

From the start, Stikkan was like a breath of fresh wind to music publishing in Sweden. He had a lot of new ideas and boundless energy to carry them out. Swedish publishing at that time was very calm and unruffled and conventional. Publishers sat around, waiting for songs to come in from abroad, then passed them on to artistes to record. It was a very sleepy way of going on: how to fail in business without really trying. Stikkan wrote hundreds of letters to people abroad, offering to translate their songs into Swedish and market them here. And while he was doing all this, he was still writing his own original lyrics at night. He was fresh, he worked like a slave, and slowly he got himself a bigger and bigger slice of the music cake. He is a human dynamo, and some years he was translating four or five hundred lyrics. It got so that it seemed every song played on Swedish Radio he had something to do with. This only encouraged him to write more and more. His best-ever record was writing six of the lyrics in the Swedish top ten. He was phenomenal, and it was not just a matter of churning out anything and some of it being successful by the natural law of averages. He really had a good nose for a potential hit.

Like most successful men, Stikkan built up a stable of enemies, and a considerable number of critics. He was totally outspoken and very controversial. Journalists got to know that a call to Stikkan Andersson would guarantee them some material which ranged from the nonconformist to the outrageous. One illustrious phrase has remained in people's memories, and is constantly coming back to haunt him. Talking about the popular music on the scene at the time, he said: 'People are not as dumb as we think. They are dumber.' He also raised many a laugh and established his eccentricity over his name. His birth certificate name is Stig, and Stikkan the nickname. Now, everybody else in Sweden who uses the nickname spells it Stickan. That was not good enough for Stikkan. He wanted to be different, and insisted on it being spelt with two Ks. Whenever he was interviewed by a journalist, he made a point of telling them how his name was spelt. It became a gimmick with him.

None of this did anything to stunt the growth of his company, which he had eloquently dubbed 'Sweden Music'. It was soon worthy of the title. The songs flowed in from all over Europe and his pen was never still. In the 1960s he had more hits in Sweden than anybody else, and by 1965 he estimated that he had written the lyrics of more than 3,000 songs.

Stikkan, who, with his moustache and abbreviated beard, still carries the studious and intent looks of a schoolmaster, recalls his struggles with a certain relish. He said: 'All the fight of the early days was worth it. It all prepared me for the bigger battles ahead.'

Those battles were to be rigorous – and Stikkan was to come out on top. Despite his country origins, he was no small town dreamer heading for the big city, expecting to find its streets paved with gold. He knew that if he was going to find any gold, he would have to make it from his own effort and expertise. By the time his biggest challenges came along, he was already a fully-fledged businessman who knew his way around the tight corners.

There was no way a man like him was going to endear himself to the established mandarins of the music world. He was rude. He spoke out. He was unorthodox. But what they feared most was that he was good. If you've got a nice sleepy thing going, what could be a bigger shock than to find an energised talent snapping at your heels? Before Stikkan Andersson, the image of Swedish music was firmly fixed to the folksy and the old-fashioned, comfortingly harmless to the professionals abroad. He has managed to change all that – and, in his way, reversed the trend. He used a lot of strange methods to claw his way up, but everybody in the business, including those whose fingers he trod on, have to admit that they admire his ability. How can they do anything else, in the face of his success?

He is incredibly egocentric. He is not modest about his energy and ability, and he has plenty of both. He was the first to advertise his 'bigness', so to speak, in magazines like *Billboard*. He is all staring eyes and shaking hands. He can't stop himself working all the time, and he is under a constant strain, because he never learned to relax.

Any perceptive person who knew him in the early days would have seen immediately that Stikkan was marked out for the big time. He was going to succeed because he had a sort of non-intellectual view of music-making, in stark contrast to the other music people in Sweden. He was very bad news to the companies which were stuck in the socialist rut, bleating that every song had to carry a social message or it was not worth a candle. A lot of these companies maintain a strong platform within the Swedish government radio by recording music with a political message, with the lyrics spitting fire at capitalism and commercialism. Stikkan has been in confrontation with them all the years. It has been a running battle, with the controversy flowing to and fro. The socialistic-minded companies and radio have heaped a lot of criticism on the so-called commercial industry, and Stikkan has come more and more to represent that side of the business. He has been the big, bad wolf, the ugly guy, and he has been in no end of fights with the government-run radio and television companies, always making his stand against the 'intellectuals' of music. His view was clear as a bell: If you give the public what *they* want, you'll sell well. If you try to give them what you *think* they want, you'll sell next to nothing. Such thinking upset the companies. He called them ostriches. He has never tried to be diplomatic in his life, and he sees no reason why he should have to be deferential or polite to anyone. He would talk straight, and it came very naturally to him. He would say exactly what he believed, and to hell with the consequences. His ego and his self-confidence always carried him through any storms his attitude threw up.

It came as no surprise to Stikkan that he had failed to endear himself to his rivals. They thought they could slight him by devising the name 'Mr Biz'. To them, it was a term of abuse, like calling him 'Mr Nasty'. To Stikkan, it was something quite different. It is typical of him that he scooped the name up and relishes it. To him, it demonstrates his rivals' underlying, but unconfessed, respect for him, and awe of him, as a remarkably astute businessman.

It was almost inevitable that Bjorn Ulvaeus should find himself being swept into the Stikkan Andersson net. Stikkan firmly believed that he had all the necessary attributes to break out onto the international scene as a songwriter and entrepreneur. He was never short of confidence. He dreamed that one day he would find an artiste or group he would be able to fly with into the heady air of international success, when he could become the international 'Mr Biz'. The first part of that dream slotted into place when Bjorn was presented to him by his associate, the wily Bengt Bernhag. The tall, blond, slender, good-looking young man could sing well, play the guitar, and had a commanding stage presence.

Stikkan now says: 'It was the chance of that newspaper article which brought Bjorn to me. As soon as I saw him at work, I knew he had great potential. They were a good group, but this boy was outstanding even in their company.' When their first record was a success on Stikkan's just-founded record company, Polar Music, Stikkan soon started making plans for Bjorn, looking for suitable material for him, and planning carefully to cultivate his career. After a short while, he confided his dreams to Bjorn – and found a mind which was a remarkable mirror image of his own. Bjorn also had grandiose ambitions of an international career, was prepared to put any amount of work into achieving it, and showed a singlemindedness which Stikkan had only seen in himself before then. The team was formed – and if the rare combination of talent, energy, and good fortune was enough, nothing was going to stop them.

CHAPTER SIX

BENNY AND BJORN

The Swedish pop community of the 1960s was a very small village. But the groups rarely met each other because they spent most of their time criss-crossing the country on a succession of one-nighter tours. It was only if they bumped into each other at the same motel that they might get together for a party.

Just such a chance brought Benny Andersson and Hep Stars to the motel outside Vastervik. And staying in rooms just down the hall were The Hootenanny Singers, including Bjorn Ulvaeus. It was Bjorn's home town, but he had decided to stay with the other fellows in the group. They met up in the bar in a flutter of polite introductions and handshakes. Over a few beers, they discussed the gossip of the business, exchanged a few jokes and stories. Then Bjorn and Benny, sitting quietly just to the side of the others, came round to the subject which really enthralled both of them: music. Bjorn offered a few opinions, and Benny countered with a few of his own. Suddenly all the polite chatter was gone, and they were deep in deadly and earnest discussion. Bjorn recalls: 'Listening to Benny was like listening to myself talk. I was amazed that we both had such similar ideas about music. We both felt that the performance of our groups could be improved immensely if only we were able to write all the music for them, instead of accepting music from other writers, which was adequate, but only that.' The studious, intellectual Bjorn and the warm, happy-go-lucky Benny had hit it off immediately. They liked each other personally, and they liked each other's ideas on music. It was a case of drifting but kindred souls meeting. Each had written songs for their own groups; on the spot they both said they would like to try writing songs together.

'Our only problem was where,' said Bjorn. 'So I called up my father to ask him if he knew a place in town where I could take my guitar and sound equipment and Benny could take his piano. He worked in a factory at the time and said he thought he could arrange for us to use an office there. He fixed that up, and Benny and I got our equipment together there and then. We loaded all our gear, the amplifiers and so on, into one of the band buses and carried it all into the office block. That was the only office block with any lights showing in Vastervik that night, and our partnership had begun.'

Benny produced bunches of chords from the piano while Bjorn sat on a stool a couple of feet away, searching for notes that would develope the musical themes. 'Our styles dovetailed immediately,' remembers Benny. 'We had both tried writing with other people before, but we knew that this time we had the right partner.'

They played on far into the night, getting together snatches of a song here, bits of a melody there; nothing complete, but each piece with a lot of promise. In the dawn hours, they had to clear out of the office to make way for the incoming workers, and also to go each his own way on the tours. They promised to get together again as soon as they could and finish off their night's work. They visited each other's flats in Stockholm – less than a couple of miles apart – to do so. Their first completed song was 'Isn't It Easy To Say?' which slotted into a Hep Stars LP. The next was 'Flower Of My Garden', which found its way onto another Hep Stars LP. 'Neither of us could read music, and we still can't,' says Benny. 'And we developed a very haphazard method of throwing notes at each other which just happened to work well for both of us. As soon as one of us spotted a few chords the other liked, we'd try to build on them. It's the only way we know to put a melody together, and it's always worked very well for us. The words were always the hardest part. They would come last, and we'd try to match them with the music. We'd try to sing the songs before we got the words, by fitting in gibberish syllables, until we could work out what words to use. If anybody had heard us, I'm sure they would have sent for the men in the white coats. Fortunately, the walls of those flats were pretty soundproof, so no-one else had to listen to our music in its very raw state.'

A couple of years after their first meeting, Benny decided to quit Hep Stars because he felt he could make headway outside the group as a songwriter and performer. He approached Bjorn, and suggested they could write more songs together, and perhaps even make records together. Bjorn took Benny to meet Stikkan Andersson, and asked what he thought of the idea. Stikkan recalls: 'I never had been able to understand how two such vastly different characters got along so well together, but the evidence of their closeness was in their music, which managed to be somehow both smooth and volatile. There was magic in their partnership. I said: "Sure, why not? Let's give it a try." ' So Bjorn and Benny set up Union Songs with Stikkan. The idea was that the two boys would produce the melodies, and all three, in harmony, would write the lyrics.

Partnerships, particularly musical ones, are probably the most difficult arrangements in the world to run smoothly, and keep together. The trio succeeded. Bjorn and Benny would tinker about with the notes, and when they came up with a melody, would sit down to play it on the piano and guitar, and tape it. Then they would start getting the phrases together for the lyric. They'd pass their ideas on to Stikkan, he would add his suggestions and a few lines and hand it back to them. Eventually they'd end up with a melody and lyrics. It was a haphazard arrangement, but it worked, and their songs were successful. Some they sang themselves, others they passed on to other artistes.

'We had to make demo records of these songs,' says Benny. 'You can't go round to see artistes and producers with sheet music and lyrics. You've got to be able to demonstrate to them what the songs are all about.'

Bjorn recalls: 'If we liked the sound of a melody we had

turned out, we'd take it into Stikkan's office and try it on his piano there. The astonishing thing to me is that during all our time of composing Benny and I have never quarrelled. We have gotten more critical about our writing but we haven't quarrelled. And when you think it can take us sometimes several days to come up with one single good bar, that is pretty good going. We must have a good friendship to be able to take that sort of strain.'

Bjorn is the exact opposite to Benny in many ways, but musically they could not have hit it off better. Benny is happy and easygoing, whereas Bjorn is the intellectual type, a guy who likes to analyse things, to talk a lot. He likes to be thought of as an intellectual type, and he has a very crisp and business-like approach to life. Benny, on the other hand, seems to be at pains to prove he is by no means the intellectual type, and he is not. Many people who like Benny because he is so easygoing dislike Bjorn because he can be pernicketty and cocky, as if he knows best all the time. Sound engineers don't like Bjorn around because of this; they think he's a bit highbrow and his manners put them off. But they all have to admire his ability and his tenaciousness. It was always obvious that he was going to make a lot of money; he's not greedy, but he's what Swedes call 'money smart'.

Benny and Bjorn, in conjunction with Stikkan, have gone on to become one of the most prolific hit song teams in history. They make the perfect team. Benny is the nice guy, the born musician. He loves music, in fact he lives for music. He's playing all the time. Even now, when he spots a piano, he can't resist sitting down at the stool and playing. And when he's not playing music, he's listening to it. He is happy, perhaps at his happiest, if he is left alone for hours with an old harmonica or an accordion. He'll play all day and be as happy as a sandboy. Benny is not interested in the money and all the trappings that go with it. He's a musician pure and simple, and it's the music that keeps him happy. Bjorn, on the other hand, is the clever guy and the organiser. Benny is the guy who comes up with the spontaneous musical ideas, while Bjorn is the one who puts them in order. It is he who decides, 'We'll do it this way,' or 'We'll make it that way.' He is the planner and the brains in their team, while Benny is the musician and improvisor. And capping the partnership is the expertise of Stikkan Andersson, who is the one who can pick up the threads and weave them together, and of course do the all-important marketing for them.

Bjorn and Benny realised very early on that they had to write in English if they were going to bite into the international market. Record producers were afraid of Swedish songs, they found, and it was easier to sell them songs in English. And Stikkan told them: 'If you write in Swedish, you will write for Sweden alone. If you want to write – and play – for the world, your lyrics must be in English. That's the international language of pop.'

The boys also found that the music they liked to write was what people wanted to hear. 'That's very fortunate,' says Bjorn. 'Because it makes us very commercial, and we still get a big kick out of writing. But that's the way it must always be. If your music is not from the heart, I don't think it can be any good. I don't believe it is possible to set yourself like a computer, programmed to turn out popular music. I'm sure you would only turn out material that sounded wooden and contrived.'

For Bjorn, life was a continual battle to decide whether he wanted to be a songwriter and performer, or a backroom boy in the music world, working out the studio production. He said: 'I sometimes feel I work best in the studio, and that the studio is the place where I should be. If I were forced to choose between singing or producing records, I would opt for producing. The stage is the place where I feel least comfortable. It's always a big strain for me to be "on". I can't relax on stage. When I go on, I have to think: "Smile! Smile!" But I can't do it very well. On the other hand, I think I have the right background to be a record producer. I feel that one day I will be a businessman in music, and, in fact, that is my long-term plan. I know I can't last forever as a performer.'

This willingness to get involved in the technicalities of the business has endeared him to Stikkan. They have built up a very close relationship and a good rapport. Bjorn's sharpened business senses and his aptitude for work, combined with a shrewd mind, have led to the Stockholm pop fraternity calling him 'Mini-Biz'. It's a suitable title, because he is second only to Stikkan in his will to fight for success.

Bjorn got his wish to work outside of the Hootenanny group during one winter, when their *folkparks* summer tour was over, but the change was not to get him offstage. He spent a few months guesting with Benny's group, Hep Stars. It led them to decide to try out a record together; they made an LP called 'Happiness', which got absolutely nowhere. They followed this up with a single called 'My Kind Of Girl'. It was a hit – in Japan. But nowhere else. They both made the final break with their two groups, The Hootenanny Singers and Hep Stars. Svenne Hedlund also decided to get out of Hep Stars, and that was really the end for the group. The drummer, bass player, and guitarist who were left went on to form an outfit called The Rubber Band. Benny and Bjorn were to survive the break, but the groups could not. With their lynchpins gone, their days were numbered.

The hits continued to roll out, mainly for other artistes, and one day Benny and Bjorn devised an incredible plan of action. They announced: 'Now we'll produce songs and records between nine in the morning and five at night. It will be exactly like going to the office.'

Benny said: 'I haven't had to keep regular times since I finished school, so it will be nice to have that discipline. Many people, I know, think our work is all fun and improvisation. Well, it's not always fun. We've been doing it for years and years now and we find it very tiring, working on to the midnight hours. It's the end of all that for us.'

Bjorn said: 'It can be fun, but you can't count on it. Nine times out of ten writing a song is something we manage only after a hell of a lot of sweat and work. We'll still work the same way – tossing ideas around between us. I think we've developed to the point now where we can offer each other some useful constructive criticism.' He candidly admitted: 'We don't think everything we've turned out has been a masterpiece, and there are some tunes which, in retrospect, we now would rather we had not written.' And, talking of their future plans, he said: 'We have strong ambitions to expand in this business, and we would like to do some film music. Writing a musical must be fascinating. We'd like to try that.' Bjorn betrayed his wariness of the stage when he said: 'I think we would like other artistes to sing our more ambitious material, and the simpler songs we would handle ourselves. I don't know what we will turn out with our new approach. I guess we'll have to wait and see.' Benny just shrugged his shoulders and smiled.

Their plans to go over to a nine-to-five day didn't last very long. They found that inspiration didn't necessarily come within those hours, and they were back to burning the midnight oil, Bjorn driven by his insatiable ambition, and Benny seemingly urged along only by his love of music.

CHAPTER SEVEN

BJORN AND AGNETHA

It was one of those Sundays straight out of the Mama Cass song: the sort of slow-moving, dreary day that showbusiness performers have learned to fear. They will claim that they enjoy the day off, a day away from work, strain, and responsibility. In fact, they usually don't know what to do with themselves without all that in their lives. Bjorn Ulvaeus switched on the radio and walked across to sprawl in an easy chair, gazing out on the Manhattan-type skyline which has imposed itself on Stockholm. The pop and ballad music droned on in succession, and Bjorn wasn't really taking any notice. It was just a background to his thoughts. Then the crystal clear voice of a young girl snapped him out of his reverie. She was singing a soft, sentimental, slushy love song, just the type Bjorn could not bear. But there was something about that voice which fascinated him. He listened all through the record, enthralled. A couple of miles away, in a similar flat, Agnetha Faltskog was listening to the same record. For a different reason, she, too, was entranced. The song, 'I Was So In Love', was her composition; and the voice singing it was hers. It was a hit by now, and she still got an excited thrill to hear her own music and her own voice on the radio.

Bjorn fell in love with that voice, though he was not to meet Agnetha for some months. He bought the record, and played it over and over and over again. Bjorn now recalls: 'It was so strange. A guy with my background shouldn't like that music at all. It was just not my style. But, for some reason, the record absolutely fascinated me. It was the voice, I guess. So sweet and delicate. Yes, I suppose I fell in love with the voice. I had never heard of Agnetha before, and I had no idea what she looked like, though I felt sure she must be delicate, fragile, and lovely. Couldn't be anything else. I played the record so many times in my flat, and even took it on tour with me so I could listen to it in my room. Looking back on it now, it amazes me that I did actually fall in love with just a voice. And the very strange thing is that my vision of Agnetha turned out to be exactly right. When I did meet her, I felt as if I'd known her a long time.'

Chance was to bring them together when they were both booked to appear on a television show being taped in Gothenberg a few months later. What Bjorn did not know was that Agnetha was a keen follower of the fortunes of The Hootenanny Singers – because he was in the group. When he walked into the television studio, Agnetha, whose boldness is well concealed by her demure looks, strode up to him, and said: 'Hello, Bjorn. I've been looking forward to meeting you. I think you're the greatest, I really dig you and your music.'

Says Bjorn: 'I knew she was Agnetha, because I had seen her on some television shows. But this sort of reaction was the last thing I expected. You could have knocked me down with a feather. I had been wondering what I would say to her after all this time. She took my breath away. Just like that, she fell in love with *me*.'

Agnetha remembers: 'I had seen a lot of their group on television, and heard them many times. I liked their music, but I particularly liked their lead guitarist and singer, that fabulous Bjorn. And when I met him, he was so nice. I remember after my forward introduction, I had a good look at him, and he was better looking than I could remember from the television screen. It was so cold waiting around for the cameras to start and he took my hands in his to warm them up. And we haven't really let go of each other since.'

Within a short while, a matter of about three months, they were secretly engaged and moved into a tiny bedsitter flat in the Kungsholm area of Stockholm, overlooking the Karlsberg Canal. In the close confines of that flat, their relationship was to have its early test by fire. Agnetha is a sweet, kind girl, but when she gets angry she is a bit of a spitfire. Bjorn was to find out, and Bjorn got to be pretty good at dodging the missiles she hurled at him when they had an argument. Most people cannot bear that sort of wild reaction and temperament. But to Bjorn it just confirmed what a fascinating and interesting person she was, someone who would never bore him. Their relationship has not changed. They are very close, and they really like each other a lot, but Agnetha has got the same sort of temperament which can send her off the deep end. Once she stopped a New Year's Eve party dead by hurling a smoked herring across the room and hitting Bjorn in the face with it. There was absolute silence for a moment, then everybody started to laugh, especially Bjorn and Agnetha. It is her way of showing she cares for him; he does not mind at all, though it is the sort of affection most of us can do without.

Not surprisingly, the rumour got around that Agnetha and Bjorn were in love. It was a disappointment for both of them because they had hoped to keep their romance secret for a while. Agnetha told a newspaper: 'I can't deny it. We are together, and we are very happy. I'm sorry we couldn't have kept it quiet for a bit longer, so we could get to know each other without any outside pressures on us.'

Bjorn said: 'We've been together for two months now, and we are in love. But we haven't thought of anything serious like engagement and so on. We want to get to know each other better before we take that sort of step. We hit it off immediately, but we want to wait a while to see if we really do like each other enough, to give our relationship a test of time.'

Shortly after, they were off in separate directions, Bjorn touring with The Hootenanny Singers and Agnetha touring with her own show. She says: 'It was terrible to be apart again. Before I met Bjorn I felt I had got to know him well through seeing him on television, and admiring him from afar. Suddenly, I was back to that, and only seeing him on television. We spent a lot on telephone calls to each other, but it was not the same as being together. I missed him so much, and because of that I got a bit fed up with the touring. It wasn't the travelling about that was the trouble. I just couldn't bear being away from Bjorn.'

They got together again to slip away on a pre-engagement trip to Cyprus, the Mediterranean island which is the legendary home of Aphrodite, the ancient Greek goddess of love. 'It was such a beautiful time,' says Agnetha. 'We strolled about like any other young couple in love. We could go where we liked, with no-one recognising us, and behave just like ordinary people for a change. But it was all over too soon, and we were back to Sweden, and the touring, and missing each other.'

When they returned, the couple did manage to spend some time together working, with a couple of television appearances, singing old Swedish songs, and making their first record together.

Their engagement was officially announced in October, 1969, and was hailed by the newspapers as 'The pop romance of the year' or 'The chart-topping romance of the year'. Agnetha and Bjorn moved to a three-bedroom flat on the quiet and exclusive island of Lilla Essenger, in the centre of Stockholm. They had to tour the town's discount warehouses looking for bargains to furnish the flat. And their romance was to continue hot and heavy. They quarrelled a lot, and they had a lot of fun.

Agnetha and Bjorn also announced a decision, which seems incredible when viewed from their present working relationship. They said they had agreed they should not work together too much. Said a friend: 'I don't know if they had worked out that couples who work together as well as live together often end up hating each other, or if they had some other motive. Whichever was the reason, they only worked together on very rare occasions and toured separately. However, when they were together they still managed to fit in some blistering arguments; but these didn't seem to affect their feeling for each other. Perhaps it is their way of freeing their relationship of tension. Despite the kippers flying about, when you see them together, you know they share a deep and overwhelming love for each other. It's written on everything they say and do.'

Summer is a revelation in Sweden. With the snows melted and the grey skies chased away, the countryside is kissed by bright sunshine and caressed by crystal-clear air. It is every Swedish girl's dream to be a summer bride. Agnetha was no exception. And on 6 July, 1971, she became a summer bride, with her handsome Bjorn at her side.

Their tours of the country had become a quest for a church they wanted to marry in. For in Sweden, couples are allowed to marry in any part of the country, without the constraint of residential qualifications and the like. Said Agnetha: 'Those tours of the *folkparks* turned out to be very useful in this way. There are *folkparks* in every part of the country, so we had the chance to search everywhere for just the right sort of church. We wanted it to be one of the fine old gothic churches set in a lovely country area. Bjorn was as eager as me to find just the right place. He perhaps won't admit it, but he's every bit as much a romanticist as I am. And we found just the perfect church, a beautiful old white building in an idyllic village setting at Verum, in Skane, Sweden's most southerly province.'

Bjorn agrees: 'It got so that we were interested in where our tours would take us more for the possibility of finding churches in the area than the actual shows we were doing. We always had an eye out to see if there was one in the area that we liked.'

That year, Agnetha, Bjorn, and Benny had teamed up to tour the *folkparks* together, more as an experiment than anything else, but it was a prophetic look into the future. Said Agnetha: 'We were quite well received, but there was something slightly out of balance; we couldn't put our finger on it, but we knew there was something not quite right. But it was a lot of fun, and I was pleased to have the opportunity to spend time with Bjorn.' Their tour was on the move right up till the day before the wedding. The couple planned to take just four days off for the briefest of honeymoons, then go back on tour.

'We had contracted appearances to keep to, and we were not going to put those off for a protracted honeymoon,' said Bjorn. 'Besides, we didn't really need one. As far as I was concerned, our time together had been one long honeymoon, anyway.'

Agnetha was driven to the church in a horse-drawn open carriage, through the thousands of people who had flocked into the tiny village, for the biggest event in its history. The local police chief had to borrow officers from a neighbouring town to help him control the crowds. Three thousand people were packed into the square in which the tree-shrouded church stood. Inside the church, three hundred guests watched the ceremony.

It was a beautiful sunny day, perfect for a wedding. Agnetha looked even more beautiful than ever when she arrived in the carriage, with two girls astride the white horses pulling it. The crowd outside were mainly holidaymakers in the area; there was a mass of summer dresses and scores of children running around without shoes on. The congregation sang two old Swedish hymns. 'In This Wonderful Summertime' and the moving 'Let The Lord Look After These Two People'.

There was a special surprise waiting for them, which was also a dream come true for Benny. He was seated at the majestic church organ as Agnetha walked down the aisle. He greeted her with Mendelssohn's Wedding March, and played them out of the church with his own hit song composition 'Wedding'. Said Benny: 'Since I was a little boy, it had been my ambition to play a church organ. It's surprising how difficult it is to do it. The custodians are very careful about who they let near the organs; I was delighted when the pastor told me it would be okay. I was every bit as happy as Bjorn and Agnetha that day. Agnetha had her dream of being a summer bride come true, and I had my wish.'

The service was very short, in the clipped tradition of the Church of Sweden, and the pastor thanked the couple for doing more for his chapel than he had done in ten years, and for giving the village the brightest day in its history. He said: 'I consider it an honour that you chose my church for the ceremony, and you have given the people of this village a memory that they will treasure all their lives.'

Said Bjorn: 'It was strange to hear him thanking us like that; as far as we were concerned, the honour was ours. He had begun our marriage with a blessing and in just the way we had hoped for.'

Their vows exchanged amidst the clicking of hundreds of instamatics, the couple walked out to a rapturous greeting from the crowd, which surged forward when they appeared. So closely were they packed around the church that Agnetha was pushed against a police horse doing crowd control duty. The horse did its best to avoid her, but the jostling of the crowd forced it to stamp on her foot. A doctor had to be called to bandage her before the wedding procession could get under way.

They were taken through the packed village, with the throng tossing confetti and blossom over them, to the White Horse Inn for the wedding dinner. At the table were thirty-nine people and one dog – Ada, the French bulldog which was Bjorn and Agnetha's pet. The reception represented a *Who's Who* of Swedish musical fraternity. The couple danced to the music of Benny Andersson and the Hep Stars and were serenaded by the Hep Stars lead singer, Svenne Hedlund, who sang 'Sunny Girl'. Even Svenne's wife, Lotta, a black American songstress, sat in on the drums. And Bjorn had to make a contribution. Stikkan Andersson, who wrote a lyric about Bjorn and Agnetha in the few minutes before the wedding ceremony, insisted that the blushing bridegroom stand on the table to sing it. The photographers who had been denied the chance to take pictures in the church took hundreds of shots of the couple at the reception instead. And throughout the reception, a crowd of hundreds of people, ignoring a gentle police request to disperse, stood outside the White Horse chanting: 'We want to see the bride and groom.' It was clear they would not go until they had seen the newly-weds again, so Bjorn and Agnetha walked out on to the balcony at the front of the inn to wave at the crowd. They were rewarded with a cheer that a royal couple would have been proud of. Said Agnetha: 'It was a stirring climax to a wonderful day which I know I will remember every second of my life, even if I live to be a very, very old lady. I was so happy.'

A hammer blow to their happiness arrived the next morning. A telephone call from Stockholm told Bjorn that while they had been celebrating their wedding Bengt Bernhag, Bjorn's discoverer and father figure, had killed himself.

It was a terrible shock, and the gloom could be felt in the hotel. It was particularly terrible for Bjorn, because he and Bengt had been so very close. Bengt had been ill for many years, and after an operation for colitis, had to wear the plastic bag around his middle. Because of this, he could not face going out and meeting people. It made him a sad, lonely, figure. He was so embarrassed by it, he avoided strangers. His life was his family, the studio, and Bjorn's career. Perhaps that was why he was so fond of Bjorn. He focused all his attention on him, and looked on him as a son. When Bjorn had a success, Bengt was so proud, always. He could not bring himself to go to the wedding because he was almost a recluse. He was afraid of people and crowds. And not being able to be with Bjorn on his wedding day was too much for Bengt. He drove off into the forest near Stockholm in his car, taking with him a cushion and a bottle of whisky. He drank all the whisky, then turned the car's engine on. The cushion he put under the exhaust pipe, and lay his head on it in a drunken stupor. He lay down to sleep there and never woke up again. The exhaust fumes killed him.

As soon as Bjorn heard the news, he woke Benny up and the two old friends borrowed a boat to row out into the middle of a nearby lake to discuss it. Putting themselves out of reach of land when they have a particularly knotty problem is a method they have used over the years. They both find that being away from people helps them think better.

Nobody knows what those two discussed out there on the lake. They were out there for hours, talking and talking. When they came back to the inn they were, understandably, silent and brooding. It was a cloud over them, and a shadow on Bjorn's happiness. He was obviously terribly shaken up, but he managed to pull himself together remarkably quickly. When one of the authors spoke to Bjorn later in the day, he could see the cold, clinical man who lived inside him. The sorrow was burning him, but his reaction now was 'Bengt is gone and that's that. I can't do anything about it.' He said that Stikkan had offered to let him and Benny take over as producers with Sweden Music in Bengt's place, and that they had decided to do it. He said: 'It's what Bengt would have wanted us to do. He wouldn't have wanted us to be frozen with unhappiness. It's very tragic, but what can we do now? The work must go on.' A friend said: 'I felt very sad at the passing of Bengt. He had the biggest ears I ever knew for finding the right songs for the right artistes. He was uncanny, and a tremendous hit-maker as a producer. He had that sort of unspoiled ear which allowed him to hear things which other people in the business missed, and he plucked the hits seemingly out of thin air. When he heard the talent in its rawest form, he recognised it and could see the possibilities. He was brilliant, and unerring in his judgement. There was no need for him to see an artiste gilded by the tinsel and trappings. A short tune, a few bars in a cold studio was enough for him. His imagination unfailingly told him the rest.'

At the moment of Bengt Bernhag's death, one of the records he had produced was sitting at the top of the Swedish charts. It was called 'Never More'. The artistes singing it were The Hootenanny Singers.

Normally accounts of suicides are not carried in Sweden because it is considered prying into the grief of tragic people. However, there were reports of Bengt Bernhag's death in the newspapers because of his association with Bjorn and because he took his life on his protégé's wedding day. It was such a poignant story that they could not ignore it.

Bjorn and Agnetha had a sad and thoughtful, and brief, honeymoon. Bjorn said he felt he owed so much to Bengt, who had taught him a hell of a lot about the production side of music. Bengt liked him so much that he passed every secret he knew on to Bjorn, without hesitation. But Bjorn is a resilient young man. He recovered very quickly and has gone on with the business of building his career. He can be very single-minded, and when he is it is an electrifying sight to watch.

After the honeymoon, Bjorn and Agnetha teamed up with Benny again to finish their summer tour of the *folkparks*, where the favourite song in their repertoire was now 'Long Live Love', a fitting wish for the future from the young couple. But Bjorn still seemed to have no inkling of the joint career which lay ahead for himself, his bride, and his friend. He said: 'When we have finished this summer tour, we will go our separate ways as far as showbusiness is concerned. We don't want to be looked on as a sort of sweet, lovey-dovey artiste couple. We both want to be recognised individually, each as an artiste in our own right. That way we won't feel that we are in each other's pockets all the time.'

Agnetha, who had already established her name by her own lights, agreed: 'It's the only way. I don't really want people to point at me and say: "That's Bjorn Ulvaeus's wife." I want to be recognised for my own ability.' It is strange to reflect that they seemed to want to drift apart in the showbusiness sense, rather than weld their partnership even closer.

CHAPTER EIGHT

ANNI-FRID AND BENNY

Another tour stop. Another motel stop. And a few drinks in the bar, maybe. Benny Andersson grinned as he thought of the people who talked of the wild, non-stop life of showbusiness celebrities. He unpacked and walked down to the bar, ordered a beer, and settled into a chair. He looked around. Just a few people there. Then his eyes settled on a blue-eyed brunette sitting across the room. Very nice. Tall. Willowy. Elegant.

When the barman came around, Benny leaned over to whisper in his ear. 'Who is that girl?' he asked. 'I think I recognise her from somewhere.'

The barman told him: 'She's a singer, too. Anni-Frid Lyngstad. She's good, I hear.'

A few minutes later, Benny walked across to introduce himself. Of course, she knew him. Hep Stars were the big group in Sweden, wowing the kids from Malmo to Lapland. She had a few young men clamouring after her in their minds, too. But all this didn't mean much to the two people sitting in the bar. 'There was nothing electric about our meeting,' Anni-Frid now recalls. 'In fact, it was a bit damp. We had a few beers, a nice chat, and goodbye, that was all.'

Says Benny: 'I didn't feel any rapport between us at all. We just talked about travelling around, a bit about the business, that sort of thing. Nothing special. Nothing very interesting. We had a couple of drinks, I went my way and she went hers. I didn't really expect us to meet up again.'

They did, a short while after, when they were both on a radio quiz show game in Stockholm. This time Benny asked Anni-Frid to dinner, and she accepted. 'I was just at a loose end,' says Benny. 'I thought it would be nice to have a chat.

We did talk, and talk, and talk. For hours and hours. Something happened, we clicked, and suddenly we were enthralled by every word the other had to say. I've never known anything like it. And we haven't stopped talking since.'

Anni-Frid by now had gone through what she calls a 'friendly divorce' from her husband, Ragnar Fredriksson, and was living in a flat in Stockholm. 'It was really a very lonely existence for me,' she says now. 'I think that Benny came along at just the right time. I didn't tell anybody about it, but these were very lonely days for me. I spent a lot of time on my own in the flat, I missed the children a lot, and I began to wonder if it was all worth it. Should I stay to try to really put myself on the map, or should I give it all up, and go to live, if not back with my family, where I could at least be a lot nearer them and see them more often. I think I missed the security of marriage.' Anni-Frid certainly was not very happy about her career at the time. She had recorded nine songs in the previous three years but only two of them had reached the charts, and each for only one week. She was doing some television work, but her material was a trifle old-fashioned, of the 'sentimental ballad' type. She said: 'I've tried pop music, but it's wrong for me. It doesn't fit my style.'

She was right, in that the sort of pop music being offered to her at the time did nothing for her. She had a fine voice, and was really waiting for the right material to come along to do it justice. She had a voice as good as any singer in Sweden at the time, and she felt upset that many other singers with worse voices were doing better than she was, perhaps because of better promotion and that sort of thing. And perhaps because she had not yet found the music which would let the public hear her voice at its best. And at its best, it certainly is fine, warm, and balanced.

On 1 April, 1970, Anni-Frid and Benny moved into a bedsitter flat in the Vasastan area of Stockholm. It was a gloomy, cramped flat on the first floor, in an old house set on a noisy through-traffic street, but it was a true little love nest. However, the cramped conditions presented Benny with a problem. He had nowhere to put his piano. The double bed took up most of the space, leaving only a small amount of room for a sofa, a record player, and a huge pile of records. This, to Benny, was like taking his arms off. He could listen to all the records he liked, but to a musician like him, that is just rubbing in the agony. But even a fanatical musician, given the choice between a piano and a bed, has to choose the bed. There was no way out, there just was not enough room. So he played a lot at the gigs. He didn't mind long shows at all. But, of course, what the audiences didn't realise was that Benny was catching up with his practice onstage; as much as he could. He had to do it somewhere.

Benny recalls: 'Despite this, we were very happy together. But I must admit I became a bit of a music pest whenever I visited a house where they had a piano. I'd be off and playing for hours. I couldn't keep away from it. I'm glad to say that our friends didn't seem to mind. I think they understood my problem. Why, this was probably the first time in my life, or at least since I was a very young boy, that I had lived in a place which did not have a piano which I could indulge myself on.' A church organist who must have known about Benny's deprivement invited him along to play on the church organ. Benny accepted with alacrity, and played in the empty church on the enormous organ for hours and hours. He said: 'I loved it. The organist may have played to heaven, but this was heaven for me.'

Theirs was to be a 'Stockholm marriage', in which the couple lives together without getting the stamp of approval from either the church or the state. Said Benny: 'It's very common in my country. I don't know if it happens more here than anywhere else, or if the truth is that we're a bit more honest and open.' Like so many couples who didn't have the benefit of a wedding anniversary, Benny and Anni-Frid celebrate their 'anniversary' on 1 April each year, studiously ignoring the fact that that date is All Fools Day. 'It's our day, and we celebrate it as happy and vigorously as any churched couple,' said Benny. 'We exchange presents and cards and so on, and perhaps have a celebratory dinner. It's always a happy day, and a very special day for us.'

The couple were officially engaged in August, 1969, at the famous and popular but improbably named 'Hamburger Bors', an elegant restaurant in Stockholm, where Anni-Frid was appearing solo at that time. Engagement time or not, the critics were as brutal as ever with her, pointing out that they considered she was hopelessly stiff on stage, although they and her colleagues had to concede that she had an outstanding voice. The problem seems to have been that she was so shy. She was totally unable to let herself go, and so looked very cold on stage.

Their romance was hailed as pop romance of the year, number two. Anni-Frid was doing long tours with a renowned pianist of the Scandinavian circuit, Charlie Norman. She had, in fact, been on a tour with him when she first met Benny at Malmo. News of their togetherness had got out before the engagement, as is inevitable in the gossip-ridden pop world. At first, Benny had been most reluctant to talk about it, and would only say: 'Yes, we are more than good friends,' which was at least a turn round of the old familiar reply. He told journalists: 'I am in tune with Anni-Frid, but marriage is something we haven't talked about yet.' It is something they have talked about a lot since, and now Benny says: 'If we thought it would improve our relationship, we would get married tomorrow. But as it is, nearly seven years later, we're content to wait. Perhaps we'll get married when we have the time. We're very busy people, you know.' They were both very busy touring in the early days, and so often in entirely different directions. But every opportunity he got, Benny made sure he could get to the town where Anni-Frid was working to spend some time with her. Fellow musicians remember the time when Benny turned up to see Anni-Frid, but in the middle of the day had disappeared. They looked everywhere for him, and were about to give up when they looked into the auditorium where Anni-Frid was to appear that night. Someone was playing on the piano, and there was no mistaking the style and the rhythm. It was Benny, catching up on the practice he was still missing out on. He never missed an opportunity.

A few months after the engagement was announced, *Aftonbladet* newspaper of Stockholm carried a story about Anni-Frid and her break-up with her husband. The article talked about the happiness which was expressed by the pictures she had taken with her husband and two children outside their villa in Eskilstuna. It continued: 'The picture of that happiness was broken when Anni-Frid made an official announcement of her engagement to Benny Andersson of Hep Stars.' It talked of the nasty comments people were making about her break-up and the engagement, repeating the stories that she left her children when she became well-known and went to Stockholm: 'They say she fled from her husband and family in Eskilstuna to work with the big boys.'

Anni-Frid protested: 'Nothing could be more wrong. I kept quiet about it until now because I didn't think it was anyone else's concern. Now I feel that in the face of the stories which I know are circulating I must tell the truth about my separation, my divorce, and my engagement to Benny. The truth is that my divorce was decided about and over long before I met Benny. Ragnar and I met regularly when I went to see the children and we talked on many occasions about our relationship and what we were going to do. Finally, we decided that the best thing for both of us was each to go our own way. It was very carefully thought out, and I know we made the most sensible decision. In fact, Ragnar and I have never been able to talk so easily together and been on such friendly terms as we have since the divorce. I found that amazing, but I've heard that that is the sort of thing that happens with other people, too. I guess we made a mistake by getting married, but we were very young at the time and weren't too clear-headed about what we were doing. So, you see, when I left my family it had nothing, absolutely nothing, to do with Benny. And I shall be so very annoyed if I heard of anybody suggesting that it had.'

Living in the two-bedroom apartment in the centre of Stockholm precluded the possibility of Anni-Frid and Benny having the two children with them. If there was not room to cram a piano in, there certainly was not room for two children – they were then aged seven and three – to run about. Anni-Frid said: 'They live a very happy and good life now. I miss them, but I must not think about missing them. I am happy with my life with Benny and I must be content that they are happy. It would be wrong of me to take them away from a home where so many things are so right for them. I am away so much of the time, and I would not be able to look after them as well as they are cared for now.' But the couple were planning to get a bigger flat, or a house, so that the children could come to live with them on a temporary basis. 'I'd hate to be cut off from the children completely,' she said. 'I hope they'll be able to come to our new place, when we get it, and visit with us from time to time. We both like having them around; they get on well with Benny. Who doesn't?' Later, they moved to a larger flat in the Old Town of Stockholm, set amongst the romantic gabled houses lovingly carved by eighteenth-century stone-masons, and the children were able to visit. 'It means so much to me, to be able to spend some time with them,' said Anni-Frid. 'It's something many people will not understand, but also something that every mother will.'

Anni-Frid and Benny continued their tours, but the strain of being apart told on them from time to time. Once when Charlie Norman, the pianist she worked with, was going up country on a tour, which was taking in some really far flung towns for which they were not being paid very much, Anni-Frid wanted to stay in Stockholm with Benny, who happened to have a few days off. She called up Charlie and suggested that perhaps she could drop out of that part of the tour, and join the troupe later. Charlie told her that if she didn't want to come with them then, she need not bother about the other tours they were doing. She stayed with Benny – and left the Charlie Norman company.

On a personal level, their relationship surprised their

friends. They have always had a very hectic relationship. In fact, it has often been as stormy as the Bjorn and Agnetha match. There was a party at Bjorn's place on Essingen one night when Anni-Frid threw some cups at Benny. He just took it all with a smile and a shrug which, unfortunately, only made Anni-Frid that much madder. But it is very hard to make the easy-going Benny angry. Their personality contrast has always been clearly lined. In a way, it is like a match between a Koala Bear and a Tiger. And, apart from the outbursts from Anni-Frid, there are other vast differences. Anni-Frid is very much the planner, who works things out carefully. In a way she is like Bjorn. Benny, on the other hand, is the opposite to a schemer. He just relaxes, and lets things happen, and does not get uptight with what is going on. Agnetha, oddly, is just like that, and loves her music, like Benny does. So the planners ended up with the easy-going members of the partnership. No doubt that is the best way, for if you get two easy-going people together, the result can be boredom. But if you get two careful planners with a bit of fire in their temperament, the answer can be all-out war.

That tiny flat also presented another problem. Benny loves to listen to classical music like Tchaikovsky and Rossini, and Baroque music. That's not Anni-Frid's bag at all. She goes for jazz music and singing. The flat was so small that it was impossible to hide from the music, and that must have produced a few clashes. But Benny must have had a bit of influence on Anni-Frid's taste in his own gentle way. They go to the opera and ballet when they can find the time.

Anni-Frid has a bit of the iceberg about her character. She is not a cold person, but she certainly is cool. There is also a strange contrast within her which makes her lazy, but also very ambitious. There is no doubt that her career is of paramount importance to her. She had a terrible time when she was in the position of knowing she was a good singer, but saw a lot of less-talented singers being more successful than she was. It did not make her bitter, but it made her that much more determined. She really had to earn her success; for a long time it seemed that she would never make it because she did not have the warmth and personality that makes a popular singer. She was a bit cold for people, and, even if she had an incredibly good voice – she is very clear, very technically correct, and can be strong or soft, in fact she sings just like an instrument – she did not have the right personality on stage to win people over. Benny has helped her get over these problems in his own way. Not by telling her. Benny is the sort of person who shows by example, the only way he knows how. She has mellowed a lot now, although she has that certain aloof air about her, just enough to give her a stage sophistication, but not enough to detach her from the audience. It is so funny to see her and Benny discussing techniques, singing, and music. She takes it all so very seriously, and he makes remarks ranging from light suggestions to outright gags. But what he has given her shows in the very impressive performer she has become.